The Hai
Lett

written by Jenny Alexander
illustrated by Tom Clayton

Mouse had a haircut.
"It looks fantastic!" he said.

But when he went to school, Tom and Danny teased him. They sent him notes in class ...

They teased him all the time.

"Don't take any notice," said Jojo.

But Mouse was unhappy. When he got home, he cried. Jojo told their Mum about the teasing.

Mrs Macdonald wrote a letter.

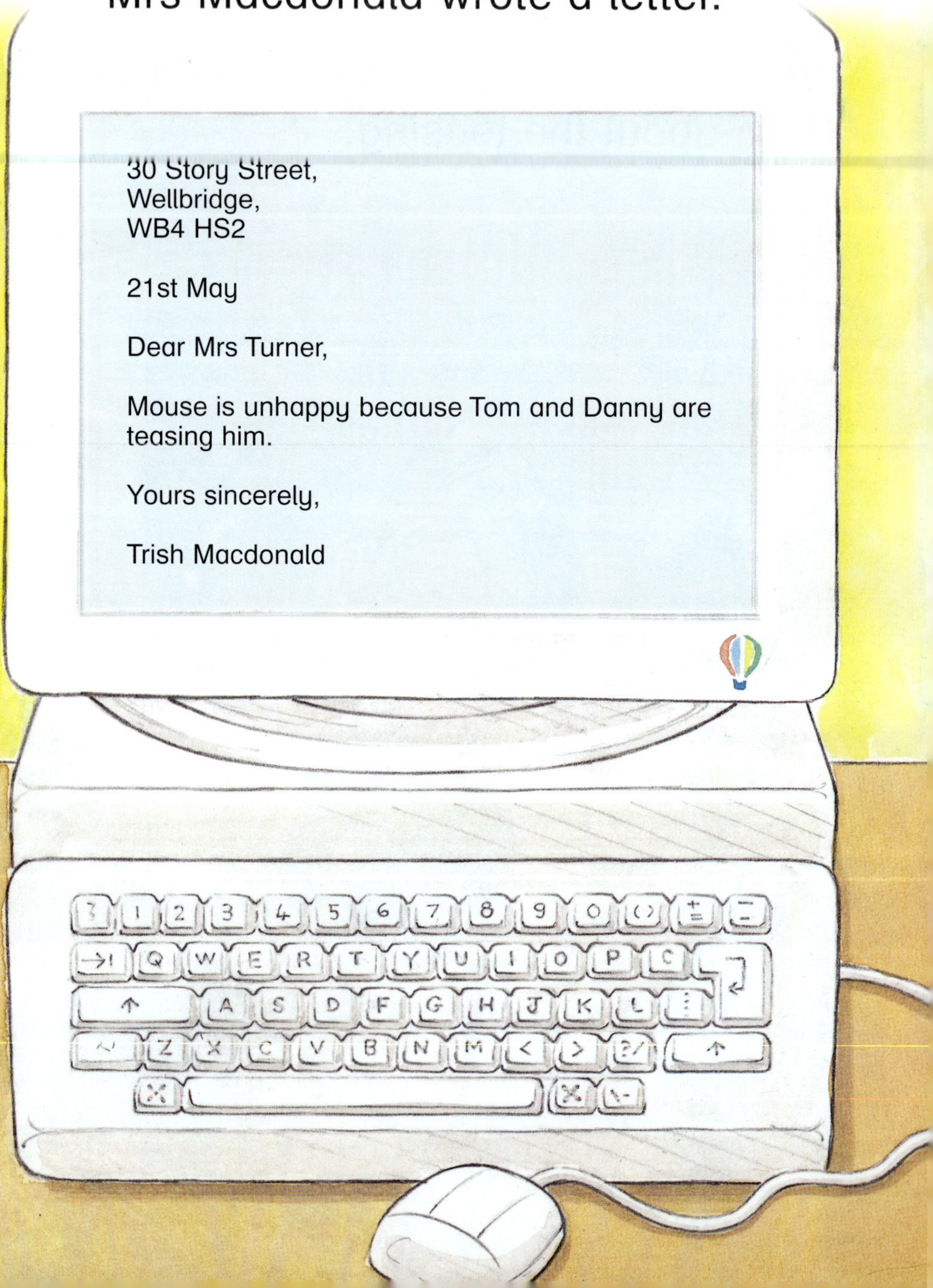

Mrs Turner read the letter, and then she gave Mouse a note for Mr Hopkins.

Story Street Primary School
Dear Mr Hopkins,
Please send Tom, Danny and Mouse to see me after assembly.
Thank you.
From
Mrs Turner

After assembly, the three boys went to Mrs Turner's office.

"Mouse is unhappy," Mrs Turner said to Tom and Danny. "Do you know why?"

"Is it because
we teased him?"
said Tom.

"It was only a joke,"
said Danny.

Mrs Turner nodded.
"That's what I thought," she said.
"You were just having fun ..."

"But now you know that Mouse is unhappy about it, I am sure you will want to stop."

"Perhaps you could write him a letter to say sorry" she said.

Later that day, Mouse found
two letters in his tray.

Story Street School

Tuesday 30th May

Dear Mouse,

Nice hair – not not!

(sorry.)

From

Tom

Story Street School
Tuesday 30th May

Dear Mouse

I am sorry we made you unhappy.

(Your hair looks ok.)

From

Danny

The teasing stopped, and Mouse began to feel better. After a few days, he wrote a letter to Mrs Turner.

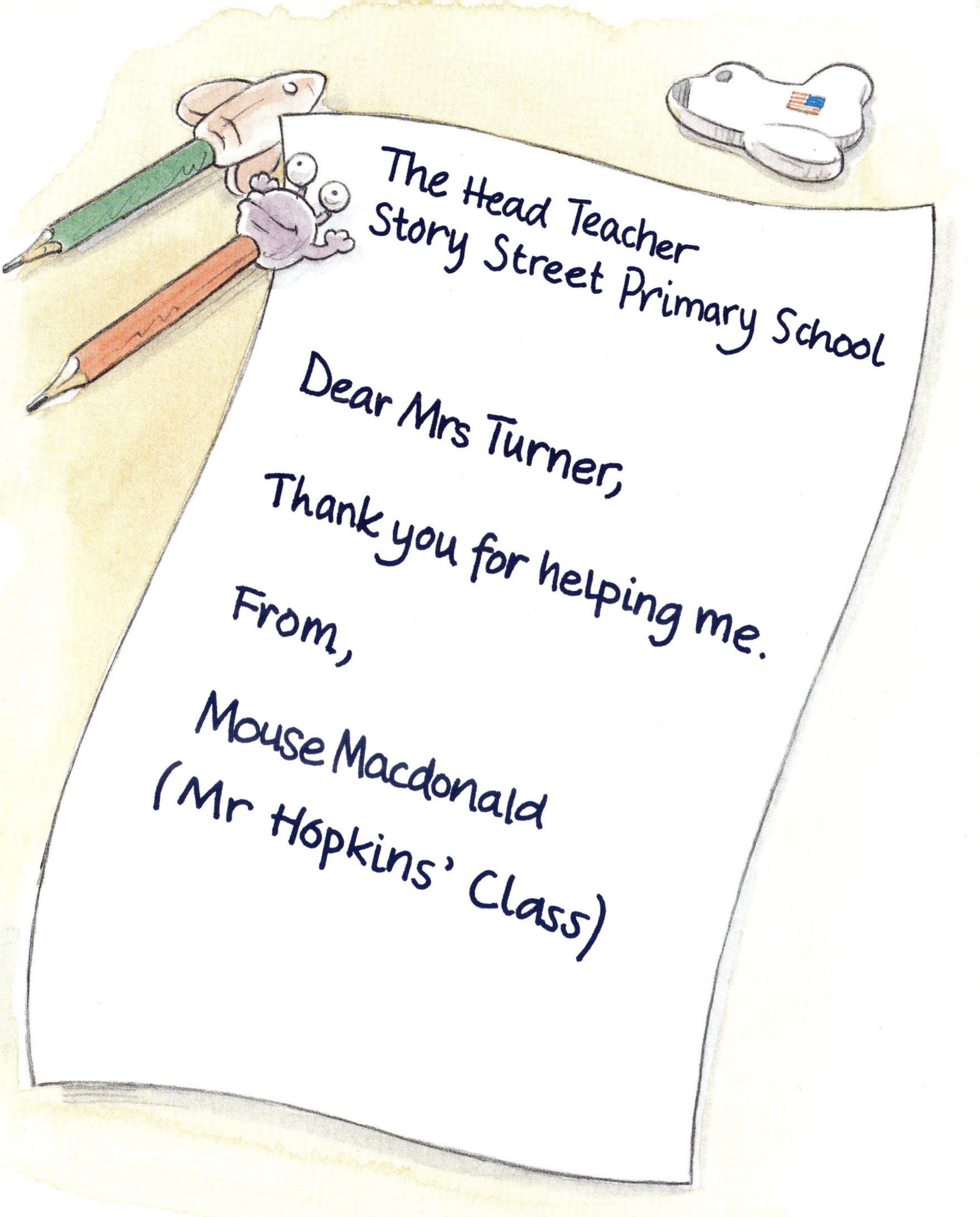

The Head Teacher
Story Street Primary School

Dear Mrs Turner,

Thank you for helping me.

From,

Mouse Macdonald
(Mr Hopkins' Class)

But Mouse was still shy about his
haircut. He hid it under a hat.

He wore his hat all the time, until ...

Dear Mouse,
Please don't keep me covered up all the time. It's hot in here!
From
Your Hair
NASA

Mouse laughed. He liked his hair again.

And when it was time for another haircut ...
"How would you like it?" said the hairdresser.
"Same again please," said Mouse.